Words in Sequence

J.R. LYLE

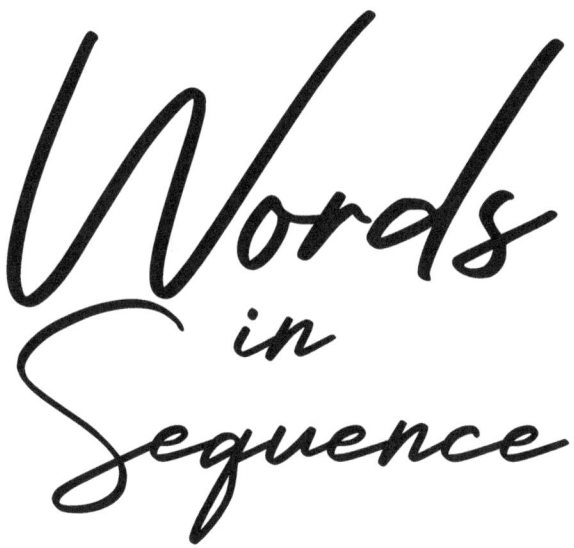

a compilation of poetry

LaunchCrate Publishing
Kansas City, KS

Words in Sequence is a work of poetry. Names, characters, places, and incidents are either the productions of the author's imagination or are used fictitiously. Any resemblance to actual persons, living or dead, events, or locales is entirely coincidental.

Words in Sequence
Written by J. R. Lyle
Photography by J. R. Lyle, Jakaila Morgan, Jamicheal Morgan
Photography Curator, Dinsdale J. L. Morgan

© 2021 LaunchCrate Publishing

ALL RIGHTS RESERVED. No part of this publication may be reproduced, distributed, or transmitted in any form or by any means, including photocopying, recording, or other electronic or mechanical methods, without the prior written permission of the publisher, except in the case of brief quotations embodied in critical reviews and certain other noncommercial uses permitted by copyright law. For permission requests, email the publisher with subject "Attention: Permissions Coordinator," at the email address below.

LaunchCrate Publishing
Kansas City, KS
info@launchcrate.com
www.launchcrate.com

Ordering Information:
Quantity sales. Special discounts are available on quantity purchases by corporations, associations, and others. For details, contact the publisher at the email address above. Orders by U.S. trade bookstores and wholesalers.

Library of Congress Control Number: 2021919196
Hardcover ISBN: 978-1-947506-24-4

Printed in the United States of America
10 9 8 7 6 5 4 3 2 1

First Edition

Acknowledgements

Life is an accumulation of sharing. As long as I can remember I've been encouraged to share. To this day, I am still encouraged to share. It is because of the relentless efforts of encouragement, validation, love and support from my loved ones, my heartstrings, my closest friends, and so many more that the journey to share becomes real.

Grateful for the many blessings, to include individuals that have been strategically placed along my path to further support this journey, completion of this work, and beginning of many more.

May we all be continuously renewed and validated with the factual statement, "You are enough."

Thank you for your never ending support.

Foremost

Photography by Jakaila Morgan

Pen to the Page

Closer to dreams
Closer than it seems
Only starving artist know
So many gifts, longing to share
Right forum
Right set
So many things for which I am unaware
The paradoxical passion from my brain to my pen
I'd run out of ink or lead
While words continue to string together within
Unable to sleep
Awakened by the sounds of verbal imagery
As a single word becomes a phrase
A phrase into a page
Of emotions, dreams, positive and negative situations or things
To breathe life into them with speech
Feels like I'd lose my breath
But my brain to my pen
Is comfortable and endless

Words in Sequence

Subtract myself from the current equations
Allowing me to feel memories
Smell past scents
Relish in special time spent
Humbling, peace
While the pages become filled
To me real this is
An expression reaching into corners of my being, my soul
I loose myself into the fabric of words
Intertwined so precise
Separation an impossibility
Joining my pen to the page even in an arthritic or trembling phase
The persuasion by passion to write
Will not be denied
Brain to hand that holds the pen to the page
Brain to the hand that holds the pen to the page
Over and over again
Until the communication between them somehow fades
Becomes jumbled, becomes senseless to those attempting to read
To me will always be
In perfect accord
Supporting a never ending journey
Brain to the hand that holds the pen to the page
Closer to dreams, I am with my pen
Closer than it seems

Indignation

Indignation is a perennial source of controversy
It latches on to every stem of your being
Infesting your life like a cockroach in a run down High-Rise
giving birth to agony, blame, and defeat
A vicious cycle of self-condemnation
It obliterates hope and suffocates love
Blind to its victims
With no name or mercy
Esteem is lost
Traveling the world with very viable modes of transport
Your verbals and nonverbal
See indignation like hypertension is a silent killer
Because although you strive to stay alive
Those internal vessels sustaining your life
Die
Enabling the nourishment of your spirit old and young
Stabbed in the heart by your tongue
Over run by this pandemonium of epidemic proportion
We learned and therefore teach

Words in Sequence

The beginning of the end
Indignation
Strangling the breath out of life
Survival presented as a myth
One way in, no way out
Forever feelin' the need to shout
To be saved
To be given something
Anything more pleasant than the obvious
A kind smile or nod of the head
    Good morning
    Good evening
That positive acknowledgement by someone
That your being exists
Still indignation persist
Always beneath the umbrella of frowns
Negativity has the tendency to drown
Because we weren't taught to swim
Just dropped in
We struggle to tread
Without guidance
Without support
Without love
There is no hope
What is life without air?
All that we teach, we're in so many ways taught
This book should be closed
We should press hold
Educate on the verbal and nonverbal cues that foster
Positivity

Reverberate

Time stamped in permanent fluid ink
A living tattoo of sorts
Running ever so slightly below the surface
Making its presence known
Basking in the light of sun-kissed skin
Her time is not His time
His time is not Her time
So their time cannot be defined
As the sharing of time escapes them both
In a place of endless possibilities
Time being the only distinguishable tangible constant
Yet remains untouchable
The voids found in choice
Revealed in fear
Repeated in the uncomfortable comfort
Render the fluid priceless marker gathered
X marks the spot for every post
Occurring or recurring
Symbolizing distance traveled

Words in Sequence

Or fencing built
A lot of experiences or lack thereof
Running forward with the exception of reflection
A choice to review
Time well spent usually defined by the associated emotion
The same way as that of time spent in regret
The illusion of control that is nonexistent on so many levels
At times seems to suggest time can be saved
Yet only in a memory is this time
For no one it waits
Continuing with or without our presence or participation
It's beauty lies in the simple fact that
Time. Just is
Still, present, active, precious, constant
If we were more like time
An awakening explosion of beauty
Painting detailed portraits of life's canvas
The joy, the pain, the love, the sadness
The overlapping layers of relationships, connections, interactions
Be in time
Do with time
Live in Your time

Cadence

Beyond the realm of significance
The redundant pauses strategically placed in the language that is shared
Emphasis to extenuate circumstances
And distinguish value

Although to each the dialect is interpreted individually
Leaving distortion to the message in its entirety

The beautiful beginning
The tragic end
Laced in the twang of a few letters
Strung together methodically

The treble note
Resounds so clear

The activity of both listening and hearing
A sophisticated art

Words in Sequence

Requiring mastery
In its truest form
Both simple
Yet
Complex

The Photo

Uniquely over exposed
Each image in His likeness
A collage of snapshots of our lives
Reveal that correctness is not easily achieved
But rather the correlation of light and focus and lenses individually impacts the perception of the image we digest
As food for thought with her eyes reflecting on the shadows of past tenses
Searching for the correctly exposed themes of life
Trying to compensate for a self-imposed flaw in our visual field
As we are intentionally trying to avoid the lighting
And cast our preferences
When likeness is the key
The correlation is
In how we see what we do
It isn't related to
The over exposed
Under exposed
Or even correctly exposed

Words in Sequence

As defined by us
The beauty of the image
Rests solely in the relationship
Of the things captured
In our picture of life

Photography by J. R. Lyle

Rain Storm

It calls offering cleansing
As it washes with each drop
The earth moans and roars
To call our attention
To awaken us to ourselves
To shed intermittent light
A glimpse on the possibilities
Offering a clean slate for the time that follows
But first cleanse
In its serenity
One with self
Reminded of the journey
Released from all that is stagnant
As the rain brings the newest of life
There is purity found in tranquility
Peace in the stillness between the drops
The detail is in the purposeful attention
To see the detail before the ground meets the drops
Forming a flowing unity
Exemplifying an accessible calmness

Words in Sequence

In a once again togetherness
Until our separation to rise
Only to come together individually
The process of healing, and growing
Beyond rhetoric
The rain and the storm
To be enjoyed just as much
As the sun that comes after

The Art of Being

Vibrant and dullness simultaneously exist
In a space of unknown or unrecognized anguish
What is to one is not to others
As we move through life
Enhanced by the aid of background coding and decoding
With touch that is not intimate
Yet somehow immensely meaningful
The unique climate within brews temperaments
That settle, rage, comply, rebel, or fly
Each robustly vibrant
Though elements of dullness create contrast
That enhance definition and character
That highlight the strongness in a feature
Or shade out the smallest perfectly imperfect imperfections
The under tones give the richness to the most poor
The texture an identifiable stimulant in areas with less light
Simply a pinpoint on a canvas
That is ever changing
With each stroke
Each breath
Each reposition
Each stance

Innermost

Before

Meaning before understanding
Understanding before meaning
Before time graced a mind with perspective
But seedlings without root
No car, no money, no diamonds
Materialistic
Even though we don't always eye to eye see
My circle completes with you and yours with me
As meaning and understanding surpass one another
As tests and trials present and we live through
What you have done for me and I for you
Simultaneous continual links
Old before new

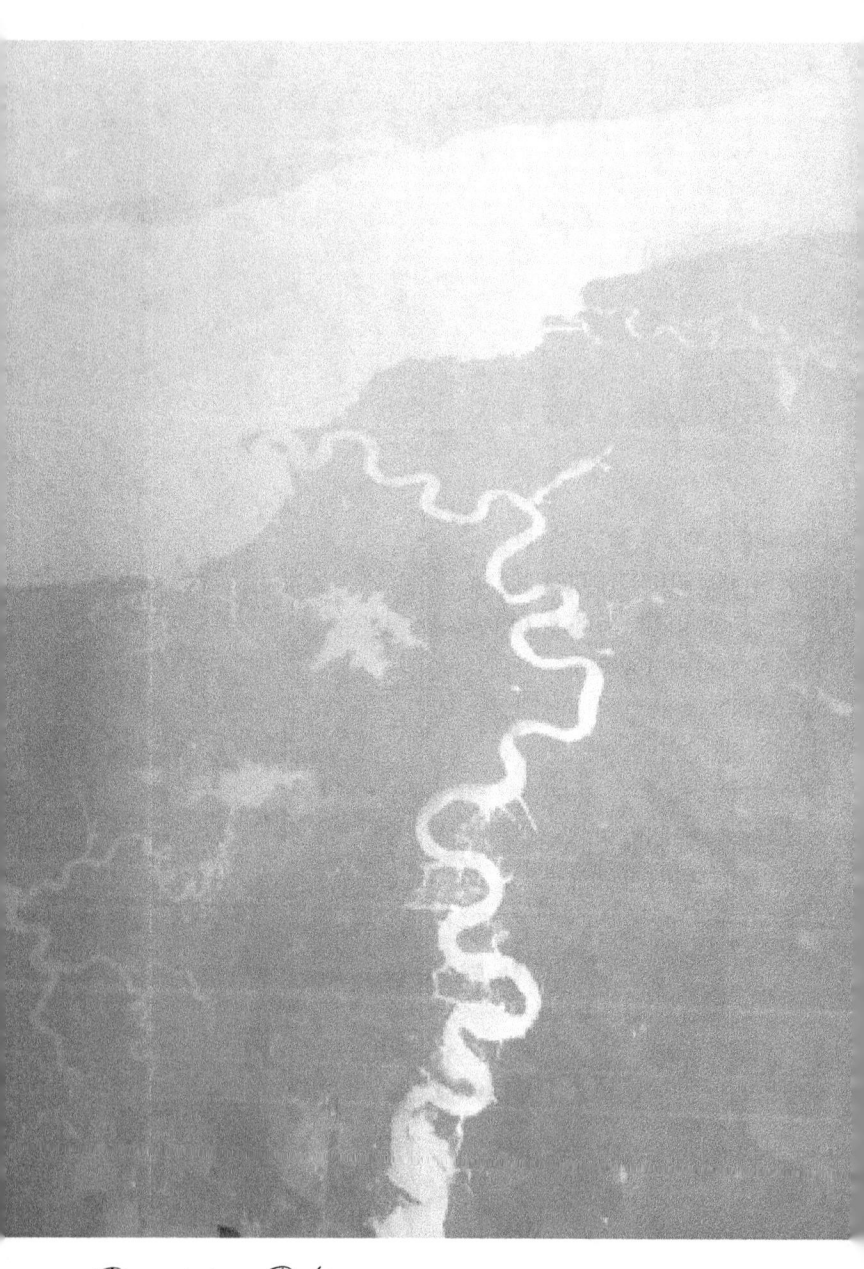

Photography by J. R. Lyle

Abyss

A child should know where he comes from
Instill in him where he belongs as he grows
For if these things she knows
She can then decide who she is and where she would like to go
Feed his mind
And nourish his soul
Overwhelm her with knowledge of opportunity as she grows
Only then will she know
Where to look
How to find
The missing pieces during troubled times
Tend to his wings when they are but little buds
So that when he is able and ready
She will soar above clouds
Uplift her in every way
Listen to things he does and doesn't say
Hold your child close to your heart
And allow your child to hold you too
Be the best friend

Words in Sequence

Be the mentor
Be the parent that every child deserves
For truth be told
No child had a choice but to exist
Teach your children where they belong
Support the notion that they can do
Don't allow them to awaken to abyss

Unfinished

Unable to foresee tomorrow
To offer recognition and appreciation seems to be precipitous
The horizontal controls so temperamental
Reflections of the now jagged past
For each step forward
The tendency to move several back seems inevitable
Round and round the same track
Literally facing forward
Yet oh so backward
The inverse relationship of the two
Stagnant
Completion illusive
The vertical climb necessary

Pay Attention

Close your eyes
Follow you heart
Take my hand
Here is where we'll start
Side by side
Laying blocks of trust, love, and honesty
The foundation
From the same cup we drink
And the same plate we eat
Nourishing the body
Replenishing the soul
In bright darkness
You feel for the textures of this journey's road
Eyes still closed
With only your hand in mine
We blindly go
Picking up everything that feels good
And toting it along
Your mind never stops turning because you just don't know

Words in Sequence

You can't see
You only feel the things you hold
Although it feels nice at this point
Your body now aches from carrying this load
You see
As you've traveled
You picked up almost everything
Afraid to pass it by or let something go
As I said before
With your eyes closed
You just don't know
So you continue to gather
And carry this increasing load
Despite the pain and exhaustion
Unsure if you're moving forward or back your mind keeps turning
How many steps you've lost track
And on top of all this
The hand you once held is no longer there
Your hands filled with something
You think feels good
And have every intention of sharing
Once you get to where you're going
Which is where you think
That person you started this journey with, will be
Still you cannot see
And now you cannot hear
That comforting voice
Silent abyss
You call with no answer
Frustration sets in

Pay Attention

In desperation
You drop everything
That felt good
When your eyes were closed
Because now you don't want to wonder
You have to know
You finally open your eyes
And look for that person to share
All the things you've been carrying
But there is no one
There is nothing
You realize
You are only a few steps away from the unfinished
Foundation
Mind still turning
Wondering if you should have
If you could have
Opened your eyes
And let something else go

Pay attention

Believe

You believe you should received
All those things they told you
You couldn't have
Resuscitating a dream
Revelations swirling
Between each synapse of your brain
Assumed insane
As the jumbled clutter
Spills from that open cavity
With no rhyme or reason
Unable to decipher the rules and regulations
Wade through that red tape
Attempting to conceive a new reality
I can
And I will
REACH to excel
To attain self-satisfaction
Giving birth to self-actualization
Believing in you

Words in Sequence

Allows someone also to
So wade through that red tape
Like it was the cleansing waters of Jordan
Submerge yourself
Your soul lifted
Welcome tomorrow again over
Opportunities endless
Believe

Altered

We traveled to the sea
On promises of prosperity
Bound by chains in conditions
Most could not conceive
And survived

We did

Instrumental in the construction
Of the foundation of this great land
This great land
Through physical, mental, and emotional captivity

We, are a part of the people, from the people

Survived
Blood, sweat, and tears
On our backs we carry causalities of previous and ongoing
War for freedom

Words in Sequence

Our freedom

A notion for which we traveled
The underground railroad
Marched many of the streets stained with our blood
Swung from most anything
Souls were more than worn
Listening to sermons of hope,
       "I've been to the mountain top"
Singing hymns of faith and perseverance
       "We shall overcome"
Struggling to be heard, to be recognized, to be educated

To count

To have the opportunity to freely choose
Overshadowed by oxymorons

Separate but equal, united

While being unable to acquire prosperity
Forced to settle on some level
For substandard quality
And still we survive

Persistence

28 out of 365 have been dedicated
To after celebrate
Hundreds of years of history

Altered

An annual motif of insignificance for which we should be proud
Corrupted by lack of opportunity
Many turn or provoked to someone's definition of violence
In a hurried less than methodical act of hopelessness
A cycle of self-denunciation that seems to continue to reign free
Family structures in disarray

Normal

Not even taking the time to recognize where we have come from

28 days

How can we continue to survive as a people
We can't celebrate and educate ourselves 365

We can

Each day a new day
Filled with many opportunities and promises
Look past
See through
Focus new
The journey is never ending
It is pursued by you

This Woman

This woman in her every shade of brown from the blackest berry transcending down
So sweet is she the harvester of life
The most precious prize, unrecognized
Still this woman she stands in the midst of it all even the most short and petite she rises big and tall
Synonymous with center in all her grace
With fine ties in shadows she hold everything in place
The pillar of love, hope and support
It's in the background she does most of her work
She has many titles and wears many hats
This woman with her crown encompasses all of that
She carries your burdens and suppresses her own
Trying to build you up constructing man's backbone
Certified in every trade by ancestral nature
Our roots are the life line for this whole population
This woman is the most valuable jewel and should be treated a such
Pampered and adored it really doesn't take much
She will discern and stand even on unsteady ground

Alone if she has to
This is why she deserves that crown
Many times knocked down trampled and more
She gets back up owning her responsibility in keeping open that door
When all else fails and there seems to be no way out
This woman in her judicious ways has to problem solve without a doubt
You see
There is no choice for a woman on more levels than we care to see
Acquisition of most by default
When she steps down from her reigns
Inevitably chaos is brought
So men lift her up and cherish her
Teach your sons to do so too
She is the most diligent harvester of life
Without this brown woman its true
There would be none of you

Grateful

I think she has wings
When no one is willing, she stands in the gaps

I think she knows beyond what is shared
When the answer before the question is formulated

I think she sees through the facades of changing faces, in smoke and mirrors
Focusing on the depth of truths

I think she senses when sense is obtuse
Recognizing a presence before an arrival

I think she tastes the bitter and sweet
Relishing in the recipe before all steps are complete

I think she connects to the finest fibers by touch
Weaving a net of safety before the face of danger

I think she...

I think she
Is
The definition of many blessings

Photography by Jakaila Morgan

Epiphany

Walking away from life to find life
To learn to live
To recapture the essence that is
To reciprocate proclivity
Unconditional
While figures become shadows
And shadows fade with the sundial
Losing its place marker
Along with its impressionable ascendancy
To breathe fresh air
And disturb the settled dust
With the art of divergent medium
Never to be the same
Embracing the deepening
Vocalize then resurgence
Treading with confidence
Into egregious joy
In the midst of infallible uncertainty
There is a light that shines

Words in Sequence

Clearly revealing a path
Journeys to be discovered
Or renewed
Anew

When

Never thought full circle would circle around on an unending loop
Generational over and under indulgence
Blinded, open eyes watching and seeing
Internal shelters of comfortable informed and educated ignorance
The pleas of unknowingly unknown synonymous with knowingly knowing
As breath is stolen, and life is lost
The art of being
Simply an unfortunate caveat to some
Unsolved riddles with clear and apparent explanations
Misrepresented discrepancies that become the structure
Callus realities like fruit from trees
Unable to prepare or forecast outcomes beyond the ever present constant loss
Impediments
Impact 2 and 3 fold
Generational stories forever changed
Some never told
The pressure that make diamonds
Bagged and toted
Shoulders hold
Eminence a fallacy systemically

Words in Sequence

When
A centuries old question without answer
Resonating in the tone
The look
The siren
The preference
The knock
The interrogation
The whisper
The clutched purse
The subjective scoring
The automatic assumptions
The cryptic overhead announcements
The guarded stance
The…
The…
The generations that will never know being without.
The
Methodical confiscation of bounty
The being
The engrained reward
What is left to give or to be taken
To be generous or selfish with
Generations
Infinite
Reverberation
Collides with existence
A vast left and right winged perception
Established by a person
When

Here

Images in the puddles and clouds
Intermingled
Or simple happenstance
Meaning in most everything can be assigned
Or
A sign
Depending on the witness
And the need or desire for explanation
Driven by circumstance
The cloak of life
Appearing and fitting differently for everyone
As experience, access, and exposure
Shape and mold the lens
Broad, narrow, near and far sight
Blindside interpretation
Fuel action and inaction
In a fast paced time
Of instantaneous expectation
Imposed

And cultivated
Unintentionally accepted
And adhered to
Socially penalized
Misunderstood
Perceived in a negative light
When opposition to this norm is exercised
Hidden meaning by the masses
Contrast the notion of peace of mind, body, and soul
Cloak of boundaries
Appropriate and lost
In the comings and goings
Interpretations and misinterpretations
Of situations and circumstances
Images for some real
Some fallacy
Some unseen
Some ignored
But here

Here

Occupying space
Thereby time
Hence valid to some degree
Images
Impressions
Impartialities
Implications
Imperfections
Imperviousness

Commitment

A bond of truth
Of trust
Of love
Of respect
Of communication
A border of adventures
Excitement and pleasures
A designated chosen confinement
To purpose and mutuality

Circle of Life

The soft touch of young yet discerning with wisdom hands
They cared as they had witnessed caring
Attentive and engaged despite the unfamiliar uncomfortable
As the demonstrators are humbled by circumstance and vulnerability
Laced relationships of value hedge a protective fence
For which supports the courage to stand, in place of,
To stand, along side
To stand, in front of
To stand, behind
In a capacity beyond their assigned years
A blessing
A validation
A labor of love
As a teacher becomes a student
And a student becomes a teacher
Commenced in a role as protector and provider
Relinquished without notice to receiver and beneficiary despite pride

Words in Sequence

Sweet joys in moments of uncertainty
Fuel strength and recovery and reason and interrelatedness
There is value in exemplifying the active demonstration of character
Transparency
Full circle
Worn rejuvenated by example
Unwearied nourished by example
The old and new
One

Reflective

As One

As one we are or should be
If we are to soar closer and effortlessly
Above the drama cloud
See through population fog
The sounds of ringing phones with complaints
Verbal aggression face to face
It's like demolition, sometimes
The remodel, others
Removing loves barriers
Confidence... oil
Security... water
As one we should be
Assembling
Rebuilding me
Over
Constructing We

Tribute

All souls deserve recognition
Despite their previous faults
We love, we remember, we cherish
And hold their spirits close

A worthy sparkle of light
To lead fellow man on his way
That brightened everyone's day

Strong willed, strong hearted, invincible love
All intertwined as one
With remarkable strength and courage
To stand firm on the ground of which one stood

So many filled with the spirit
To flourish onto others
The memories of their joy, love, and laughter
will always shower upon us from above

What is It

What is it that everyone has to have
Or have had
Blind to the socioeconomic class
To the gender or race
A prize in disguise
Overlooked by so many
Over run by trials and tribulations
Mere existence maybe taken for granted
Irreplaceable rays of Caribbean sun
Because there is only one by definition
Many more by interpretation
Helping to unlock the doors to life
A parameter of love as you step forward
Or back
Never diminishing
More sentimental than your first memorable accomplishment
Knowing without
You would not be
Strategically woven in your thoughts

Words in Sequence

Your personality, your speech
Your entire composition
A forever present readily accessible disposition
Think
We all should know
Without it the world couldn't go
Despite the portion that fit in a pot or mold
This you are told
Be kind and mind
As far as can be traveled across the globe
So you don't have to go
Be proud, feel privileged

Done thinking
What is it's that everyone has or had to have had

    A mother's love

Tainted

Ever seen a place tainted with tantalizing temptations
Forbidden yet so excessive
Cross over or turn back
Limited invitations only
Acceptance, refusal
Tantalizing temptations draw you near
Fear of uncertainty bleeds you here
Damned if you do damned if you don't
Temptations so sweet you'd be a fool not to want
Sweetness has various degrees
Each tongue savors differently
Sweet can be bitter Bitter can be sweet
Stop, Go
Yes, No
Stand, Sit
Twirl around flip over
Jump High, stoop low
Hold on
Tantalizing temptations will have you spinning all around

Words in Sequence

If you let it
If you test it
If you misconceive and believe
If you become wrapped in its silk web
You will be consumed by the mere thought
A better place a better way

Ever seen a place tainted with tantalizing temptations

Probably more than you care to say
But the real contemplation is
Do you cross over or do you turn away

Ambitious Man

You are my ambitious man
Ambitious man you are he
Fighting tooth and nail
To excel
But eyes closed to your surrounding life
At what price
My ambitious man
Ambitious Man you are he
With will power tough as steel
Encapsulated in a segregated mind
Separate but equal
Holds no aspect of truth even at this time blinding ambition
Paralyzing ambition
Dividing and conquering ambition
You are my ambitious man
Truly truly you are he
At what price will you pay
For your ambition today
You are driven, obsessed, and consumed by one cause

Words in Sequence

Is ambition truly ambition when you choose to weave your silver lining of life with a single strand
Are you my ambitious man
Are you truly he

Dark Chocolate

Dark chocolate collage
With several hues
Drifting in a distance
A mirage
So close
Still unclear to me
My eyes through the sand storm
Just cannot see
The heat has dehydrated this body
Filled with fine abrasions
Not quite deep enough to bleed
The stinging seems to supersede
Actual pain
I can't remember wishing for rain
To flush my eyes
Quench my thirst
Cleanse my wounds
Drop the temperature of my own personal earth
Just one cool subdued drop

Words in Sequence

Enabling me to submerge my inner most thoughts
From this illusion I am freed
Now welcoming the breeze
In a distance
A distorted hays
The anger inside me
Fuels visual heat rays
When I think about
The dark chocolate
I willing to taste
Agreeing with medical experts
It's better for you
I wish I could erase the bitter taste
Plastered across my desert sky
Like the stars
Each one unique
Usually a pleasure to the eyes
That seem to collect tears
When you are near
Because you're really not here
I'm basking in the sun
With no water no shade
So hot
Emotions surfacing through my pores
Evaporate
As I gaze into the chocolate hues of you
I realize
This I can no longer do
The desert filled with scripted delusions
Of you

Dark Chocolate

Or us
Or what I'd hoped we'd be
The mind is a powerful thing
The rain finally falls
The breeze now feels cool
Because I've realized
I possess a small paradise
Without you

From Wince We Came

The reason you are is
because we were
And they were
and they did
and they had
and they and they and they
And you
You take the best pieces from all the fragmented
Disjointed associations
Of personalities traits, skills, strengths, and abilities
To cope within
the gift you try to suppress
and they
And you
And we become blended in the daily expressions of who you are
and they were
And we
And you
can't do anything in a silo

Words in Sequence

because from where we can grow to become
And know
and share
and give
and take
and give back to those
No one knows the struggles and pain's that are intricate in us
That in you trace back a breadcrumb trail through the generations of
you
and we
and they
We say, from wince we came
It doesn't have to determine where you will go

Never Forget

The strongness in your voice
Stern but comforting
The expressed desire and demonstration of covering
Felt even now
In the absences of physical presence
Ever so real
The power of never ending influence
A bond without full explanation
Levitating fire lit patrol
For which the meaning is never truly understood
Until roles transition
The immense awakening
Methodical decisions and movements
Reflecting on what struggles and pressures
Time and situation demand
Great expectations relentless
Challenged to strive even when you've reached the top of society imposed standards
To set your own bar beyond that

Words in Sequence

Laced with stoic emotions
I know now
A camouflage
I understand now
What I didn't then
The intention to build armor
For the world can be cruel
And there would be times when
The love couldn't cover
And hands could not reach to defend
Or preserve the emotional health or innocence
Prominence and memories
Stories that rest within your vessel
Your treasures
Treasures build the wealth of legacy from the root
Lace the veins in a way
Fortifying a deep connection of existence
Lighting a pathway full of unknown influence
Empowerment
The impact of such a repository
Perpetual
As each absorbs the portion that uniquely strengthens
The gaps on their strands as they do life
I see you more clearly each and every day
I understand the treasure you gave me
Intended to be shared
The responsibility to simply stand for something
Not just anything
To actively drive towards it tirelessly
To consider family a gift to be protected and valued

Never Forget

Never forget your stillness on the surface
Your constant work behind the scenes
In your eyes I see beyond me

He Loves Me

He loves me more than the breeze loves the blow behind it
without it
the winds are
stagnant
what is breath without air
He fills me with a whisper so faint yet loud
professing His love if I choose
to stand
In the space uncomfortable for a moment
To catch the lesson hanging in the barometric pressure of the
atmosphere that is me
loving
immeasurably
He stretches over and over
again
Inviting with soul-searching acronyms
And refurbished moments in time
Captured and defined by the stares as
He holds me

Words in Sequence

Free from the effervescent white noise
just the opposite of purity
He sees with my heart
        as my eyes are closed
He knows
The depths of my breath can not sustain me alone
ask Him
He is the blow behind the breeze
The nourishment above the supplement
The Cause supporting the Be
He loves me

Synonymous Affinity

Memorizing Forever

I traveled to a place with passionate emotions
I journey through a valley surrounded by mountains of joy
I bathe in the water of kindness, and tasted the water of spirit
Viewing the exotic lands baring pedals of love
Listening to the sounds of a heartbeat ringing,
        echoing deep down within me throughout the land of
        beauty
My heart, beats the same beat
My voice sings, the same tune
Engraving everlasting, memories forever of a place and venture
Holding them in my hands ever so tight
Keeping them fresh in my heart
Locking the doors after every memory enters
I'm taking a journey through love gaining memories to last forever,
building a timeless bond
I'm traveling to a lake of passion in which I find contentment
I'm traveling to a loved one
I'm taking a journey through you

Feel You

Can I feel you
Can I caress you
Inhale you
Savor your aromatic essence
Your presence sends lukewarm vibrations through me
I can only reminisce
Like a fingerprint no one is the same
We fit
Mesh
Able to filter the noise
Your heart beats the rhythm of mine
Oh so much time
We've spent
Wasted the royals of love
yet still I interpret your blink as a sensuous line of poetry
The curve of your lips an intimate proposition
The force of your exhalation calling me
Come here
Let me feel you

Words in Sequence

Place my fingertips adjacent to those that already exist
Though with the naked eye cannot be seen
With every touch a perfect match
Untainted like a map of predetermined destinations
With eyes closed you will go never missing a step
Post and regain composure
Inhale satisfaction
When you mesh
There is no other attraction

Hold Me

Hold me today don't let me go
No tears.
The thought of your presence comforts my soul
The things you mean to me you may never know
Promise this connection will never grow old

Travel with me miles of open road
Beneath blue skies, holding me with your eyes
Extract this frame
You do the same
Come travel with me

When you're away I can still feel your touch
Hear your voice as though you were here
I am wreaked in our memories
Unable to separate truth from fallacy
In my mind so much time
Reality demands something that seems so short
My heart
I wish you could see
For right now, come travel with me

In My Skin

I smell you in my skin
Feel you in my dreams
Hear you when the wind blows
Perspiration laced with the scent of you
In your absence, constantly reminded of a connection
This more powerful than a single thought could fathom
The heart is in dysrhythmia as it tries to capture the tempo of yours
A fusion of harmony created as they run together
In my mind, able to admire your detailed sketch
And faintly caress the sculpture that is mine indefinitely
In my skin I am every moment
Previously reminiscent

No Other

There is no earthly love that can surpass
The love that a mother or grandmother has
So many burdens she bares
Not only for self but everyone else
Preparing and guiding your thoughts and steps
Propelling you forward to grab something else
Humble and smiling even during hard times
Her wisdom and comfort always seems to bind
From generation to generation
She left her mark
We all have our special moments because she was there from the start
Without judgment without phase
She responded to our needs from day to day
In Jesus name she prayed that we would take heed and rest in His safe arms
From Sunday morning breakfast and the journey to church
To kickball in the streets back on Birch
Our lives are more Grand for you having been here

Words in Sequence

Emerged in our lives from afar and near
As you held our hands, and spoke words with your eyes
We felt your love one last time
In the midst of our sadness we will hold on to your love
Remembering all the times we've shared together, all your smiles
The tenderness of a hug

Love Is

Love is unconditional and everlasting
The voice you hear telling you it will be ok
That uplifting embrace
That encourages you to go on
An extra something even though you didn't ask
Feather tainted kiss
Warm intimacies
Only two people can share
Surrounded by a cloud but oblivious to the scenery
You and Me
You and Me
Love is unconditional
And everlasting
Reassuring, dependable, faithful, and dedicated
Through and through
Floating without wings
Or even a breeze
Suspended in space
Timeless
Effortlessly
Natural attraction

Love Is

Addict

I lose my breath when your image dances through my thoughts
The way we talk
And talk
And well
Talk
An instant addict high
I experience with the presence that is you
Oh, I do relish the orgasmic pleasures
A simple thought from your every amenity
We are like birds of a feather
Or ice cream and cake
Flying high and ever so sweet
As the whispering breeze carries you and me
As we explore new land and fancy.... new opportunities
Who knew happiness exists in the simplicity of free flowing
uninhibited verbal expressions
In our mosaic of differences
The commonality of
Just being

Words in Sequence

Just breathing
Just seeing me for me and you for you
All that we do that is unnoticed by so many
Speaks volumes to us
Between us

Speak

Words that speak to my soul
Without the auditory stimulation from speech
Combing the knots from my entangled thoughts
As they continue to grow
An untamed mane
You soften my edges
By deep conditioning
Me
Forever present
Your image is with every blink
I see you more clearly
Barriers and unanswered questions
Lending a hand to division intermittently
Yet still as I dream with my eyes open
I find myself in a hypnotic trance
Stumbling over thoughts
Wondering among much else
Are you wondering about me
Memories tattooed throughout the corridors of my mind

Words in Sequence

For which you will always have the key
Like therapy you massage the wrinkles from my inner turmoil
Releasing the tension from my brow
Lengthening my vertebral spaces
As you lift the weight from my shoulders
Standing tall I am
Relieved by the presence of you
My upright posture is boisterous
Allowing the poison of frustration
To escape with exhalation
Stunned and wavering in the joy
You bring me simply by the way you be
Content while fulfilling my list of needs
Continually in metamorphosis
No worry or sound consistent with compliant do I have
Hard to believe all of this
Even from a distance
I possess a distinct clarity for a gift such as this
So little yet so much you give to me
Without the presence of mind to suggest
A notion of negativity
Forever uplifting my spirit
You nourish my wellbeing
Fueling me
For those unexpected uphill journeys
I am tireless because of your positivity
We are bound by Ivy vines
Providing a haven for intimacy
As I am loving you and you are loving me
And we are together loving we together

Speak

All of this to make you aware
Have no confusion about the ties we have tied
Nor should you worry
2020 vision could not reveal the details
Of the inscription of emotional bondage
For you I do
Speak in languages for which I have no background
In an attempt to express
Similarities in you
Your eyes tell me
What your mind and mouth cannot come to a consensus to say
Pupils constrict
Supporting...
Suggesting...
The introduction of a glamorous light
For which I am to you
And you are to me
And we are together

We speak without making a sound

Transient Affliction

Imagine

Imagine darkness
Lonely without the scent of your being
Silence
Echoes of respirations
Hovering clouds of despair stop
The new life that lives
The other growing more each day
Constant struggle to provide needs
While may go unnoticed but not away
Still must link one to the other
Strong ties
In darkness keep strolling through
Darkness is thick and piercing
Within hearts
When eyes open with hopes of your vision
Only darkness a cloud, a shadow of fear
Confusing lingering and near
Open windows and unlocked doors
Pause

Words in Sequence

Imagine heavenly bliss
Your warmth through the night
A smile a kiss
All of which are missed
Showers of affection
Beams of happiness
Rays of joy
A wonderful breeze tainted with whispers of love
A sigh
My my my
A prayer
A dream
A reality
A possibility

What's Wrong

Can you tell me what's wrong
What happened to this love usually roaring strong
Raging like a river
It's bed full of eroded stones
Like the corner of my heart
The mosaic of intermingled bits and pieces
Colors and shapes
Encapsulate my mind
With each glimpse breathing life into my spirit
Just like the source
That raging river
Taking note it only runs forward never to look back
Or undo
Once again I say to you
What's wrong
Knowing it's not with me but with you
To have such power, such force
The ability to carry a floating vessel overflowing with packaged love,
hate, tears, lonely days, and fears,

What's wrong I say, what's wrong
When you have so much love
But you're drowning in that same raging river
Full of life and able to carry you wherever you want to go
What's wrong...
I think I know...
Unable to love in the reciprocal.
Unable to go back and undo
We become the eroded stones that fill life's bed
As the raging river flows on
What's wrong
What's wrong

Once

There once was a time
Love me love mine
Reminisce, filtered images fill my eyes
Eyes full open wide
Cascading memories like the force of a waterfall
Infinity
You and me
Thinking planning
Life altering steps
Who knew
Love hard
Love long
Stay strong
Me and you
You and me
Never realizing all that was wrong
Or simply ignoring it
I shudder to think present tense
Where would we be today
If the day before ignore we did not

Words in Sequence

And instead listen to those nearly silent whispered in our heads
Is this love real
To stay
To go
Not knowing or caring
Not listening or mending
The water in my eyes
It all withers
Purposely stealing away
Leaving void
The water drips
Then pours
Despair a sea found by streams
Your eyes no longer hold my reflection
Fades blues
To love once

Cried

Tonight I cried
I didn't know what else to do
I never knew the depths of love
Until I met you
My heart is heavy
My mind is swirling
Tonight I cried because of you
I can't explain the extent of my emotions
My wants, my needs,
My dreams, my thoughts
All holding me tight while, swaddled
My lonely self aches more with each passing fragment of time
The tears are streaming
To the point I can't see
I never thought there would be a challenge unmet by me
Tonight I cried
I cried because there was nothing else I could do

www.ingramcontent.com/pod-product-compliance
Lightning Source LLC
Chambersburg PA
CBHW060102230426
43661CB00033B/1399/J